COLLECTIVELY WRONG

LISA JOHNSON

First Edition

ISBN-13: 978-0692833315
ISBN-10: 0692833315

Other books written by Lisa Johnson:

Morality Within the Framework of Reality
Patterns of Peter and Paul
The Evolution of Good and Evil
The Mobbing of Jesus Christ

CONTENTS

Part I
Individualism vs. The Common Interest

In writing this book, I have come to the conclusion that the concept of human rights should not exist and would not exist in a world that operated at the level of logic. After all, how is it logical that a species of human beings so alike in their individual make-up receives such disparate individual treatment? The logical truth is that the battle to create a level playing field in the fight for human rights is a battle that need not be fought at all in a world where each individual human being is operating at the level of logic where truth resides. This book attempts to tackle the issue of human rights at the level of reality and truth.

Operating at the level of reality and truth is becoming increasingly difficult in a world that has been set up for success based on man-made belief systems like competition and hierarchy because at the core of competitive systems fighting for supremacy (whether it be an individual, a business or a country) is the idea that we must keep our strategies close to the cuff for fear that if we give them away we lose our competitive edge. The end result of this conditioning is that we are now operating in systems that require more and more deception and secrecy for their survival. The winners take all in these systems and the winners are the ones who can play the system best. Unfortunately, the people who play the systems best are rarely, if ever, the best people. More often than not, they are narcissistic, cutthroat and unaware human beings playing a game they make it their life's goal to win. That is what happens when you pit human being against human being in systems built on foundations of competition and nationalism rather than cooperation and teamwork.

As counter intuitive as it may sound, the concept of fighting for human rights serves the interests of the power structure. How can people ever come together when engaged in a fight? The war on drugs. The war on terror. Religion's war for our souls. They are all just different versions of the us vs. them competitive mentality that has plagued mankind since its inception.

I became very interested in human rights after my own rights were stolen from me by a group of managers, executives and colleagues in my workplace (one of whom was the general counsel and chief ethics officer of the company). The mobbing campaign they conducted against me is a barbaric practice but what made this experience particularly difficult for me was the fact that I worked in communications for a forward-thinking company with a list of values that included respect for all employees, open communication, safety and integrity. This was an international company with locations around the globe, not some small, family run company; yet the managers and executives, including this so-called ethics officer, had no problem with treating me like an object for their abuse. The reason? I blew the whistle on one of the vice presidents who was covering up his incompetence and negligence by trying to get me terminated before a memo I drafted came to light and got all of them in hot water.

The experience and aftermath were nothing less than horrific. I began suffering from symptoms of Post Traumatic Stress Syndrome and harboring suicidal thoughts as a direct result of their actions. The silver lining was that it heightened my desire to determine what made them act in such a callous and brutal manner. What I have discovered in all my research is that bullying is not merely an adolescent problem, as if it ever was. Bullying and targeted mobbings are a worldwide problem that we may all have to deal with at some point in our lives due to the globalization of the workplace, government and society as a whole. That thought in and of itself is terrifying because unless a person has been a target of this kind of abusive behavior, it is very hard to imagine what bullying and mobbing does to a person's psyche. I certainly had no idea what mobbing-style behavior can do to a person's mental state before becoming one of its victims. It is psychological violence and torture that stays with the victim forever but is forgotten by the perpetrators as soon as they accomplish their goal of ridding the victim from their midst through isolation, exclusion, lies, scorn, character assault and a host of other strategies (if you can call them that) to accomplish their goal of turning everyone against the targeted person or persons.

Any research in the area of bullying and mobbing will naturally evolve into research on human rights because at the core of the behavior is one person denying the rights of another person to live as he or she chooses to live. It is an intentional choice to destroy the happiness and wellbeing of another person for one's own motive, whatever that motive may be.

Mobbing and bullying strategies were in fact what made Hitler's campaign against the Jewish population so successful. In Nazi Germany, those strategies were used to change people's perceptions so that eventually all Jews were perceived as wanting to destroy Germany and Hitler and his Nazi party were perceived as Germany's savior. In my workplace, I was turned into the villain and my teammate was the hero who fed them the information they needed to adjust their lies and strategy for getting rid of me before their malfeasance came to light.

Like Jesus' own traitorous colleague and friend, Judas Iscariat, who sold Jesus out for a few pieces of silver; my teammate sold me out for her own upward mobility within the company and the perks that went along with it. She served the function of the blockleiter in Nazi Germany which had neighbors spying on neighbors and reporting their activities to the local S.S. These people did not become spies overnight. Hitler and Joseph Goebbels, his Minister of Propaganda, created a massive communications machine that touched every area of German society. By the time they began rounding up Jews in the Final Solution, these members of the blockleiter thought that what they were doing was right. From their perspective, the Jews were the villains who had caused all of Germany's problems; hence the name the 'Final Solution.'

So many of us have chosen to turn a blind eye to the truth that what constitutes good and bad is a matter of perception rather than morality. Good and evil are man-made concepts that can be too easily manipulated to serve an individual or group's self-interests, as Hitler so masterfully showed us. Hitler always framed the persecution of the Jews in terms of handling the Jewish problem. All human rights violators portray their targets of abuse as the problem and then use their more powerful position in the relationship to convince everyone else that the target is the problem as well. A non-conscious population that does the cost-benefit analysis based upon their own self-interests in any given external environment, rather than basing their decisions upon an internal set of values and rules that they will not compromise, can easily be convinced that betraying the trust of their colleagues, neighbors and friends is in their best interests when the people in power control the information flow and can pass laws which make it detrimental for them not to do so.

If we were to identify the strategies used by people to manipulate truth for purposes of gaining an advantage, then we would be on the path of eradicating the concept of evil at its core and preventing any further human rights abuses from ever occurring. After World War II ended, the allied forces attempted to do just that. However, instead of identifying the core causes of the holocaust so that similar human rights abuses could be prevented in the future, the allied forces did what governments always do to address a problem. They formed a commission. The U.N. Commission on Human Rights ("the Commission") was convened on January 27, 1947, and given the job of codifying a set of human rights that would be applicable to all peoples of the world. The countries of Australia, Belgium, Byelorussia, Chile, China, Egypt, France, India, Iran, Lebanon, Panama, Philippines, Ukraine, USSR, United Kingdom, United

States, Uruguay and Yugoslavia were all represented; with Eleanor Roosevelt of the United States acting as chair of the Commission.

Almost immediately, ideological differences erupted between representatives from the Communist nations and those from the United States and the other nations with more Western democratic traditions. The representatives from the former Soviet Union, Yugoslavia and China argued that the common interest is more important than the individual interest when coming up with a list of human rights, and delegates coming at it from more Western democratic traditions argued that the rights of the individual should be emphasized.

As chairperson of the Commission, Eleanor Roosevelt adopted a very diplomatic stance by not taking sides in the argument. She adopted the view that both outlooks were equally viable, explaining that they were merely ways in which government was structured: "Many of us believe that an organized society in the form of a government, exists for the good of the individual; others believe that an organized society in the form of a government, exists for the benefit of a group."

Ms. Roosevelt was beginning with the assumption [as all the delegates were] that government is what keeps a society ordered, not the individuals themselves living in accordance with a universal and absolute set of principles they will not compromise. She tried to get the delegates to use language in the Declaration that would allow countries with these differing views of government's role in society to achieve the economic and social rights set out in the Declaration in different ways. It became a very contentious process in which each side stuck firmly to its ideology. The same arguments were raised over and over again causing Ms. Roosevelt to become extremely frustrated. The differences between the two sides were never resolved, and in the end, the representatives from the USSR, Byelorussia, Ukraine, Poland, Czechoslovakia, Yugoslavia, Saudi Arabia and South Africa abstained from voting on the final draft of the Declaration when it ultimately took a very individualistic stance in its language.

Ms. Roosevelt's failure to achieve consensus should have been a sign to her that something was wrong. The continual adding of amendments should have signaled to her that further evaluation and clarification of the vision may have been required. Although I can certainly understand the frustration she felt in not achieving consensus so that she could complete the assignment she had been given, rushing the assignment and thereby failing to get all parties to sign onto the Declaration has been disastrous in terms of achieving the vision. Holocausts, ethnic cleansings and human abuses of all kinds abound in our current global climate. I am not saying that a paper document would have prevented this outcome, but getting the full consensus of all nations involved in the process certainly would have provided a more solid foundation upon which the vision could be achieved. It could have laid the groundwork for achieving a global consensus on what it means to be a human being living among other human beings who are equal in the way they come into this Earth and go out of it, but somehow find such inequality among one another in the in-between time.

I believe the root of the two conflicting world views the delegates on the Commission held stems from a differing perception of reality. Collectivist philosophies that focus on the common interest tend to view mankind as a large group of physical beings occupying a physical planet who require structures with levels of authority like hierarchy and varying forms of governance to organize them and maintain order. In contrast, individualist philosophies view mankind as the whole of all human beings who have in common with one another the individual ability to reason and feel and can use those inner abilities to create order both within themselves and with one another.

Perhaps Ms. Roosevelt should have pushed the nations arguing for the common interest into defining exactly whose common interest they were so vociferously trying to protect at the expense of refusing to recognize the rights of each individual human being the Commission was trying to serve with its Declaration. If she had, I am quite certain she would have come up with the same answer I come up with over and over and over again in my research and daily when I read the news. There is no such thing as a common interest when it comes to human rights because human rights can only be applied to the individual human being.

The worst human rights abusers in history have found solace in the common interest. When we value the group, there is always someone else we can point our finger at when we abuse our own power to harm another person. The entire reason that the mobbing against me in my workplace was so successful was because the employees involved in the mobbing willingly abrogated their individual humanity to serve the interests of a group of executives who felt threatened by a letter I wrote. The common interest of the management team was threatened in that particular environment, and I was individually destroyed in order to protect their common interest and keep them in power. That is how so many of us lose our humanity – in deference to the collective. One of the most striking aspects of the Nuremberg trial transcripts is all the finger pointing going on. Rare were the witnesses who took individual responsibility for their actions and did not blame their Nazi superiors for commission of atrocities their own hands carried out. Their finger pointing was the same finger pointing going on in the Bible's Garden of Eden allegory. Adam points his finger at God (truth itself) for putting "that woman" in the Garden with him and Eve blames the snake for making her eat the fruit. This finger pointing strategy to avoid personal responsibility may give one a personal sense of mental peace for doing something wrong, but it is a false solace and peace of mind which has been obtained on the back of human suffering since the dawn of mankind.

To make this strategy for avoiding personal responsibility a little more relevant to our modern age where we are in the midst of a war that our politicians have declared on terrorism, let me relate to you a story that made headlines not too long ago. A student in Pakistan was writing a blog on women's rights. On her way home from school one day, a group of militants stopped her bus and demanded to know where she was sitting. They shot her in the head after other students on the bus pointed her out. When I heard about it, I began to wonder whether I would I have been one of the people doing the pointing if I found myself in a similar situation. Can I truthfully say that I would not let fear for my own life overtake me? What would prevent me from giving into the temptation to save my own life at the expense of another person's life?

These are questions I should have begun asking myself a very long time ago so that I would know the answer. I was not on that bus, but I could easily find myself on a similar bus under similar circumstances. What will I choose to do? Will I have someone killed just for being who they are because I am too afraid myself of being killed for who I am? Will I have the courage to stand down and refuse to comply to a murderer's request? Who will protect this girl and other people like her if not people like myself? The government wasn't on that bus with her — only her fellow students. The company was not in the corporate office with me when I was mobbed and my life changed forever; only my colleagues and managers. What if all the students had failed to point her out? They probably would have all been shot. Would that be a preferable fate to knowing that your own finger played a role in getting someone shot in the head? For some of us, it would. For others, it would not. Still others would rationalize that it was not their finger that pointed her out. It is a choice that each student made for themselves, just as it was a choice that each of my work colleagues made for themselves and that the witnesses at Nuremburg made before taking the stand at trial. It is always a choice. Positive change will come in our world when we all agree on how those choices get made and each of us, individually, chooses to make the right one.

The goal of commissions like the U.N.'s Commission on Universal Human Rights is to codify right choices and belief systems. Although they make for very good posters to put up on walls, these attempts to codify human behavior have always fallen short because human behavior is not determined from reading a list of articles, values or commandments handed down from people who have made themselves the arbiters of human behavior. Human behavior is learned behavior that must be reinforced with action over and over and over, again and again and again.

From the time Moses carved the Ten Commandments into stone to the time the countries of the world came together after World War II to ink The Universal Declaration of Human Rights, human beings have been drafting mission statements, constitutions and declarations of one form or another in their attempts to bring groups of human beings into alignment with one another under a similar set of values. The reason these documents fail is because they do not have the resolve of the leadership behind them to reinforce their contents over and over and over, again and again and again. The excuses are numerous. It is too laborious. It is too costly to the bottom line. We will never be able to get everyone to agree. More often than not, however, the reason these guidelines get tossed aside is because an individual's or group's self-interests are in conflict with them and the individual or group happens to be in a position where they can ignore or change them to rules and guidelines that are more self-serving.

Practice makes perfect when it comes to learning new behavior. The managers and executives in the Human Resources and Ethics departments in the company where I worked were all proficient users of the strategies of the mob to silence the truth and they used these strategies with ease because they had become so accustomed to them. These managers and executives were not told the unwritten rules when they were first hired. They accepted their positions thinking one set of values would be propagated, but quickly learned how the game was really played once they were on board. That is how it works and it is what makes corruption so insidious and ugly.

At some point in their tenure, those managers and executives had to make a choice as to whether they would follow the ethical guidelines and value system the company used for branding and recruiting, or whether they would follow the leader and sell out their subordinates and themselves by following the unwritten rules that protected the hierarchy and themselves as members of that hierarchy.

You can have people swear on all the bibles you want that they promise to follow all the ethics policies that are in place, but the reality is that unless quality people are in place to begin with, the slope will always tilt in favor of the self-interests of those with power. There is no way around the fact that you need an educated and values-driven population as a whole in order to have ethical organizations. There must be people in place who will uphold the rights of all individuals within the organizations. Our current populace, unfortunately, does not fit the bill and that is why the family man who felt it important to send his kids to a Christian private school could treat his kids one way and treat me entirely different in his role as the ethics officer of a global corporation. His own self-interests hung in the balance.

Very similar in wording to America's Declaration of Independence, Article One of the U.N.'s Universal Declaration of Human Rights reads as follows: "All human beings are born free and equal in dignity and rights. They are endowed with reason and conscience and should act towards one another in a spirit of brotherhood." There are three assumptions underlying this first article, namely (1) Birth entitles each of us to equal dignity, rights and freedom; (2) Every human being is individually born with reason and a conscience, and (3) Our individual reason and conscience can be used to act towards one another in a spirit of brotherhood. This article clearly recognizes that human rights are an inherent and indivisible part of being born human. They are not something we should be made to fight for or defend. They are the natural law guiding mankind at the level of the individual soul.

It turns out that in terms of human rights, government is completely irrelevant. If government exists for the good of anything, it certainly does not exist for the good of achieving human rights for all or they would have been achieved centuries ago. As I will attempt to prove in this book, Ms. Roosevelt's assumption that government is what keeps a society ordered, not the individuals themselves living in accordance with a universal and absolute set of principles they will not compromise, is wrong. We deny the reality of what it means to be human by believing we need a government to control us through the command-and-control structure of the state. Each of us has a command-and-control structure within our own minds that we can access and use rationally and logically to take care of and protect ourselves and others. We are not ants. We are not animals. We are the spirit of life with a human consciousness quite capable of creating the life we were sent here to create in freedom. No one can do it for us. No one should ever do it for us. We have the right to do it for ourselves as human beings born equal to one another in reason and conscience.

Part II
The Evolution of Human Consciousness

When you view mankind as a collective of physical human bodies who must be brought under the control of the state for purposes of unity and peace, then the state, rather a person's reason and conscience, becomes the unifying force. With its focus on the physical aspect of humanity as a collection of human bodies needing to be controlled and ordered, collectivist ideologies keep humanity in a perpetual state of survival from a structural point of view. Governments like those that Eleanor Roosevelt described as existing for the benefit of a group essentially assume the role of the Queen of an ant colony keeping the masses of citizenry in line through levels of authority. The common interest has to necessarily default to the interest of the people in power because there is no role for the individual in such a structure other than conformance to the state.

We are now at a stage in our evolutionary consciousness where we have the ability to move beyond the organizational structures of the animal kingdom. We are not like a colony of ants where the worker ants forage for food and resources (industrial) while the soldier ants defend the colony against attack so the worker ants can do their work in peace (military) and the queen ant controls it all from her perch at the top of the hierarchy (government). The military-industrial-government complex is very real and very dangerous in my opinion because it keeps mankind from progressing out of its animal stage of existence under the guise it is advancing technologically. To the extent that the Western democratic traditions are breaking down in the name of globalism, there could very well be a time when the concept of individualism is completely eradicated and the animal structure of the military-industrial-government complex becomes a reality for all of us on a permanent basis.

There is perhaps no greater illustration of the difference between collectivism and individualism than the Bible story of Moses and the Israelites. In the story, the Israelites were slaves who were physically led out of slavery in Egypt by Moses, but who were unable to cast off their slave mindset in order to create a new life for themselves in freedom. The Israelites that Moses brought out of Egypt had all been born and raised under an authoritarian hierarchy of slave and master where they were viewed as no more than worker ants doing the bidding of the power structure in place. Their days, hours and minutes were controlled by persons other than themselves. The concept of self-determination was unknown to them.

After leaving Egypt, they found themselves in a wilderness as far as their minds were concerned because they had no masters telling them what they should do, when they should do it and how. They were lost because they never had the opportunity to nurture their reason and conscience while under the thumb of their Egyptian masters who told them how they should think and act. What was right was what their masters determined was right and what was wrong was similarly determined. Moses gave them complete freedom, but he was unable to give them back their reason, intuition and consciousness of true and false; all of which had long been silenced by following the orders of their authoritarian masters. Although Moses freed them from the structure that made all of life's decisions for them, he was unable to free them from the internal mindset that viewed that structure as real and good. Exodus 20:19 says that after Moses gave them the Ten Commandments, the Israelites told him, "You speak to us and we will listen, but do not let God speak to us, or we shall die."

The Ten Commandments Moses brought down Mt. Sinai are the laws of God because they are the laws of a human mind that wants to protect other people by controlling its own mind, not theirs. They are the laws of the individual soul. They are the commandments of a mind that sees the wisdom of doing unto other people as it would like done to it because it sees the commonality of all human beings as thinking and feeling beings rather than as ants who need an authoritarian-structured hierarchy to keep order for them. After having spent their lives being told how they should act and treat their fellow human beings by other people with authority over them, the Israelites were simply too afraid to take that responsibility upon themselves. It would be like telling a group of assembly line workers that they are now in charge of the company, or maybe more to the point, it would be like a Democratic country overthrowing a dictatorship and telling the people who have lived under the dictatorship all their lives that they are now free to choose how to run their country without giving them the mental tools and knowledge of how to do that.

The Bible describes Moses as old and tired. Instead of digging in and giving the Israelites the knowledge they needed, Moses became tired of all their grumbling and complaining about being hungry and at least having food on the table in Egypt. (Exodus 16:1-3, Numbers 11:4-6) Moses caved into their complaints and their desire not to follow the Commandments of consciousness. He gave them exactly what they were accustomed to in Egypt by creating a structure in which they were familiar navigating. The 600+ regulations comprising Mosaic law controlled their behavior down to the hour and minute of each day. The Israelites chose to voluntarily enslave themselves with Mosaic law when the personal responsibility of freedom proved to be too great a burden.

Moses gave the Israelites exactly what they asked for and it cost him his soul. In Deuteronomy 3:25-28, Moses tells the Israelites that after asking God for permission to cross over into the promised land beyond the Jordan, God told him he was angry with him on account of the Israelites:

> "Ah, let me cross over and see the good land beyond the Jordan, that fine hill country, and the Lebanon! But the LORD was angry with me on your account and would not hear me. The LORD said to me, Enough! Speak to me no more of this. Go up to the top of Pisgah and look out to the west, and to the north, and to the south, and to the east. Look well, for you shall not cross this Jordan. Commission Joshua, and encourage and strengthen him for it is he who will cross at the head of this people and he who will give them possession of the land you are to see."

According to the story, Moses died without ever having entered the promised land because he failed in his mission. Moses had the vision, but he failed at the execution. Eleanor Roosevelt lacked the vision, but was determined to achieve execution, even if it meant failure in getting Saudi Arabia, South Africa and the USSR and its allies to sign on to the Declaration.

The Israelites were in the wilderness of freedom for forty years. It took an entire generation to die out before they were able to enter the promised land. Humanity is still waiting to cross over and will continue to wait until each and every delegate, lawmaker, boss, teacher, citizen, wife, mother, father, brother and human being born into this world is able to embrace the vision and follow the truth with faith that it will lead us individually and collectively into a world that is good for all because it is good for each one of us individually without exception.

The Bible cannot be understood correctly unless it is understood exclusively as concerning the condition of our minds. When we open the Bible, we should do so with the understanding that the physical people and physical lands described therein have absolutely no relevance to the message other than as a means of helping us to understand particular states of mind. For the slaves freed by Moses, the wilderness they spent forty years in was a representation of the state of their minds between the time they escaped from their slavery in Egypt to the time when they self-determine their future in the Promised Land.

For Jesus, his forty days in the wilderness was representative of making his mind free of ego concerns so that he would be totally prepared to follow his consciousness of truth in the thoroughly corrupt and evil environment he was about to immerse himself in. He knew he would be teaching in a temple controlled by the corrupt Pharisaic hierarchy who used the 600+ laws of Moses to keep the Jewish population under its thumb. When Jesus tells them in Matthew 5:17 that he has come to fulfill the law, he is talking about the Ten Commandments of Consciousness Moses brought down the mountain that had all but been lost in the minds of the Pharisees. The Pharisee priests were experts in stealing, killing, using the Lord's name in vain, lying, covetousness, hypocrisy and making a god of money. Just read Matthew, Chapter 23, to get a taste for the kind of men Jesus was dealing with. He knew he was going to be speaking truth about the scriptures to the corrupt power structure and it was something his mind had to prepare for in what the Bible describes as his wilderness journey.

We all wander through the wilderness when we are in the process of making positive change in our lives. The wilderness can be a very scary place when our personal resources begin to dwindle and the outcomes of our endeavors are uncertain. It can become extremely tempting to revert back to the structures that do nothing to fulfill us, but at least provide us with the sense of safety and security that familiarity breeds.

The growing pains of an individual or organization undergoing change are real. Most of us like to feel like we are in control of our lives. When external conditions beyond our control make us realize we actually have very little control, the desire to retreat back to what we know can be overpowering. In a sense, my workplace persecutors saved me because they would not allow me to retreat back to what I knew. They blocked all doors in order to protect themselves. They would not allow me to find a decent job, rely on any colleagues for support or maintain a sense of confidence in myself and my abilities. Saying I was good at what I did would not support their lies and they needed their lies to protect themselves. I was forced to live outside my comfort zone in my own wilderness and it practically destroyed me because it stripped me of all the mental and emotional cues I had relied on before to live my life. In the end though, it saved me when I decided there was no going back. If I was ever going to feel normal again, I would have to create a new mindset in order to create an entirely new life for myself.

Our individual lives are filled with land mines and sometimes they even explode on us. Unfortunately, there is no way of avoiding many of them but we mustn't be so afraid of them that they paralyze us into stasis. Our real nature as a human consciousness controlling the energy of its emotions and thoughts requires us to get up and fight another day.

Organizations are nothing other than individuals tasked with a common mission to achieve a particular organizational destiny. An authoritarian management style within a hierarchical organizational structure provides the ultimate environment for stasis of the organization and the individuals within the organization. I think more than anything else, the story of Moses and the Israelites' journey in the wilderness as told in the Books of Exodus, Leviticus, Numbers and Deuteronomy, shows us how the use of laws by an authoritarian-style governing structure is the result of a failure of strong leadership with the backbone to stick to the stated mission, vision, values and guidelines no matter what.

Moses made the Israelites suffer in the wilderness far longer than they needed to when he opted to give into their fears by implementing Mosaic Law. It wasn't until the Israelites were able to work through their mindset of dependency and fear that kept them bound in slavery even more than their physical chains that they finally realized the promise that eluded Adam and Eve. but which Jesus fulfilled for us through his teachings.

It is extremely hard to look inward in order to bring our minds in alignment with the laws of a human consciousness grounded in reality and truth. It is so much easier to just go through life assuming we are good people. Self-analysis does not come naturally. It is something we need to be trained in on a continual basis. What seems beneficial to us needs to be turned upside down (and right side up in the process). But first our thinking needs to change. As the Israelites prove to us, looking at one's situation realistically and honestly is probably the most difficult process one may ever have to undertake. In my own case, it took several years of daily study, research and self examination to come to the truth. I had to come to a place in my own mind that was completely clear of all rationalizations or justifications of one sort or another. Some are easy to spot and others, particularly those in conflict with the picture one has of oneself, are painful to acknowledge and destroy. However, this process must take place if one is to achieve a state of mind with the ability to remain constant through all the ups and downs of one's life without caving into the ever-increasing pressures of man-made external environments with values and belief systems that run counter to a consciousness of reality and truth.

Part III
America - An Experiment in
Individualism Gone Awry

Amerıca held such promise at its founding and if not for slavery, it might have gone in an entirely different direction and fulfilled its vision. But you cannot put forward a set of ideals and promises of freedom and liberty for all, while at the same time denying them to some. Slavery was the equivalent of a whole-scale mobbing. We fought one of the worst wars history has ever seen to change direction, but the wounds have failed to heal because we have never confronted it honestly as a nation and apologized. The races continue to see the issue through their own lens. Many Americans view it as something their ancestors did that has nothing to do with them. It is like all mobbings. The participants are able to avoid responsibility by finger pointing and blaming others for it; thereby no one takes responsibility and the target is the only one who suffers waiting for an apology that never comes. We are all a part of the nation which compromised its values for profit. It is never too late for an apology and an apology must be made if

America is to break free of its corrupt past and move to the next level of growth and real prosperity. Until then, I believe we are condemned to exist as a divided nation because that energy lives on and continues moving in the same negative direction. All our positive energy that could be going toward building a unified nation has been turned inward in the mode of self-protection. It is like a marriage where a spouse cheats. Once that bond of trust is broken, it is extremely difficult to get it back. No one can believe us when we say we stand for human rights and yet we never made amends for the rights of the people that were stolen for so many years under slavery and its aftermath. If we had confronted our wrongdoing early on and convinced people of the benefit in discarding their prejudicial views in favor of internalizing the truth that ALL men and women are created equal, we would have had no need for civil rights laws to counterbalance the lingering prejudice and racism in our society.

You could say that America was an experiment in individualism gone awry. It was a stand against the denial of the truth that all men and women are created free and equal in dignity and rights. It was an attempt to break free of the burdensome structure the King of England had created by corrupting the natural laws of mankind to further his own self interests. He enriched himself and his monarchy by inflicting burdensome laws and taxation upon the colonists. What follows are excerpts from America's own Universal Declaration of Human Rights: the Declaration of Independence from the King of England:

> When in the Course of human events, it becomes necessary for one people to dissolve the political bands

which have connected them with another, and to assume among the powers of the earth, the separate and equal station to which the Laws of Nature and of Nature's God entitle them, a decent respect to the opinions of mankind requires that they should declare the causes which impel them to the separation. We hold these truths to be self-evident, that all men are created equal, that they are endowed by their Creator with certain unalienable Rights, that among these are Life, Liberty and the pursuit of Happiness. That to secure these rights, Governments are instituted among Men, deriving their just powers from the consent of the governed. That whenever any Form of Government becomes destructive of these ends, it is the Right of the People to alter or to abolish it, and to institute new Government, laying its foundation on such principles and organizing its powers in such form, as to them shall seem most likely to effect their Safety and Happiness. Prudence, indeed, will dictate that Governments long established should not be changed for light and transient causes; and accordingly all experience hath shewn, that mankind are more disposed to suffer, while evils are sufferable, than to right themselves by abolishing the forms to which they are accustomed. But when a long train of abuses and usurpations, pursuing invariably the same Object evinces a design to reduce them under absolute Despotism, it is their right, it is their duty, to throw off such Government, and to provide new Guards for their future security.--Such has been the patient sufferance of these Colonies; and such is now the necessity which constrains them to alter their former Systems of Government. The history of the present King of Great Britain is a history of repeated injuries and usurpations, all having in direct object the establishment of an absolute Tyranny over these States. To prove this, let Facts be submitted to a candid world."

What follows the paragraphs above is a litany of regulations and laws the King imposed on the colonists for purposes of keeping control of the colonies in the hands of the monarchical structure under which the King of England ruled. America's Declaration of Independence was an attempt by the colonists to create a blank canvas upon which they could build the world they envisioned building for themselves in freedom. Another group of people who had the same vision and desire to create a blank canvas upon which to build a new life were the enslaved Israelites that Moses led out of Egypt. The problem that America's colonists ran into was the same problem the Israelites ran into on the blank canvas of the world outside of Egypt. The colonists and the Israelites may have physically freed themselves from the structures keeping them in chains, but their minds remained. They fell back on to the familiar when they encountered the fear and anxiety that always accompanies foundational change. The Israelites begged Moses to create the same structure they had as slaves in Egypt and the colonists fell back on what they knew when they realized the canvas was not as blank as they thought it was. Instead of working with the natives who were already occupying the land to learn the best ways for thriving in their new world, they relied on the divide and conquer mindset they carried over from Europe. The lofty idea of equality for all they inked on their own Declaration was barely dry when they began denying equality to huge swaths of the population. How different it could have all been had they internalized those founding documents and actually lived the values and ideas contained therein as soon as the ink was dry.

The Isrealites would have avoided forty years in the

wilderness if each one of them would have recognized the wisdom of internalizing their own Universal Declaration of Human Rights in the form of the Ten Commandments Moses brought down the mountain. The first of those commandments was to not have any gods before the LORD your God. The only God we as human beings can ever be sure of while we exist on this constricted and finite physical plane is the God of our limitless and eternal mind. We must believe that we were given a consciousness with the ability to reason and feel for a purpose and we should see the wisdom in following its commands with faith that a consciousness grounded in reality and truth will take us individually and as the whole of humanity to where we need to go.

A consciousness of truth and reality is the antithesis of a consciousness shaped by external environments that use branding, political correctness, advertising, spin, manipulation, lies, propaganda and various forms of pressure to make us conform so that a false consensus can be achieved in the name of the common interest (a/k/a the greater good). The Ten Commandments, the Universal Declaration of Human Rights and the Declaration of Independence were all meant to be rules that would give each of us the best means for taking care of ourselves individually and tangentially for the community as a whole. The reason all three documents have failed to achieve the vision that inspired them is because documents are only as good as the people to whom they are given.

Moses, America's founders and the delegates on the U.N. Commission for Human Rights coming from Western Democratic traditions all held a personal philosophy that is very difficult to apply to the group. They can draft all the declarations, commandments and documents they like and it does not matter. They are all bound to fail when it comes to execution because achieving the vision underpinning these documents requires that each and every individual embrace the vision for him/herself. Unless each and every person is made to see how it is in their individual and collective interest to embrace the vision, then documents like the Ten Commandments, the Declaration of Independence and the U.N.'s Universal Declaration of Human Rights will always be exercises in futility.

John Adams said, "The American Revolution took place in the hearts and minds of the people long before the first shots were fired. Their leaders inspired them with visions of independence from monarchical rule – a type of government they frequently called tyranny."[5] What Adams was describing is a change in consciousness. The reason most revolutions never work and always end up with just another corrupt group of people taking power is because the root of the problem remains. Part of the reason why the American revolution succeeded was because the revolutionaries immediately went to work putting the ideas that inspired the revolution down on paper and building a framework for the new government based on those ideals. Even though some of the founders were unable to live up to the ideals in their personal lives, the Constitution and Bill of Rights at least provided a structure for moving forward and preventing the chaos that happens in other revolutions where there are no rules to guide the behavior of the victors.

When certain presidents make the argument that the Constitution is no longer relevant, what they are saying is that the ideals upon which America was founded are no longer relevant. When people ask why Americans still rely on an outdated set of rules like the Constitution, they are not speaking in a vacuum. There are many lawyers, presidents, government officials, judges and businessmen in America who agree with them. So let me be so bold as to answer them.

Rules, like those found in the Constitution, are necessary for creating a level playing field for all. If the rules become a hindrance to winning, then unethical players will always find a way around the rules. Just ask Lance Armstrong. After all, everyone was doping. In order to win, according to Lance, you had to dope. The people running our governments and corporations use the same kind of distorted reasoning, they just use a more legal route to set up the board to win. They do it with money, incentives, promises of prestigious appointments and undeserved promotions and chairmanships. As people who play by the rules get pushed aside by people who have been able to buy their way into the game through connections, influence, power, money, or a combination of all four, then the level playing board begins to tilt in the favor of those in power who were able to buy their way into power.

The founders of America knew that the country they envisioned could only work with an educated and ethical population. But the populace must be educated and ethical. They must be taught the values and rules in the form of the Constitution and Declaration of Independence. They must be given the knowledge so they can see the logic in following them. There has been a purposeful effort to take this kind of education out of the schools. We should all be asking ourselves why. The only reason these documents ever turn from writings in stone into living documents that can be changed is because someone, somewhere finds the documents too burdensome and hard to get around in trying to get what serves their own self-interested agendas.

The mobbing against me in my workplace could not have taken place without people like the HR manager who told me that money is what motivates people to act; not some set of values or a company's mission. It could not have happened without people like the general counsel and ethics officer who accused me of being mentally unstable for reporting the misconduct of a person in his management circle. It could not have happened without people like the HR vice president who shut my manager up when she told him I voiced concerns over the team leader's abilities because the team leader was a vice president who was considered above reproach. It could not have happened without people like my manager who after hearing this from the HR vice president refused herself to help me at every turn, and in fact actively participated in the mobbing in order to protect herself. It could not have happened without people like my two teammates; one of whom pretended to be a friend in order to obtain damaging information on me and the other who called me a traitor for telling the truth. And finally, the mobbing definitely could not have happened without the puppet master at the top of the pyramid directing these people to act in the immoral and unethical manner they did.

They all lived in the land of the gray where absolute rules like company values and mission statements are living documents that can be changed when they do not further the self-interests of the people in charge. They all lived in the wilderness of their own minds where the right thing to do changes with each situation (translate: in accordance with what laws need to be avoided and what ethical behavior needs to be ignored to serve the self-interests of themselves and the power structure they belong to in the form of management).

The wilderness is where so many of us are all living now because all absolute standards of conduct have been eradicated in the mistaken belief that no one has the right to impose their own standards on anyone else. That is a lie. It was never a matter of one person imposing their own standards on another. It was always a matter of having a set of rules and values for humanity to follow so that we all lived orderly, peaceful and fulfilling lives in a world populated with other individuals doing the same.

The Bible sets out standards of conduct, but these standards become very inconvenient for people who want to do what they want to do to serve their own interests – which is most all of us. We follow the standards that are easy for us and disregard the ones that don't give us what we want or let us do what we want to do.

The stone the builders rejected has become the cornerstone according to Psalm 118:22. The stone the builders of our world rejected is the commonality of our human consciousness. That should be the foundation for building a world that is good for ALL because it is good for the ONE. The foundation is wrong and always has been wrong. The good news though is that we create the foundation. If the human race were to come up with a universal set of values and rules that respected the dignity and value of each individual equally, regardless of their race, color, creed or any of the other cultural or physical distinctions that currently define and keep us apart, and were to begin instilling these values in their children from birth, we would begin to see the world get turned right side up.

Turning the world right side up and inside out is ultimately what the story of Moses and the Israelites is all about. Moses did exactly what Eleanor Roosevelt did when she rushed the process and made the delegates put the Declaration of Universal Human Rights to a vote without consensus of all the parties. Moses made the Ten Commandments that the Israelites were too afraid to follow null and void when he allowed man-made Mosaic laws to replace them. He re-enslaved his people with hundreds of laws that dictated their every word and action, Moses should have stepped aside and let the Israelites battle it out. If they decided to pack up their bags and go back to Egypt to be slaves, so be it. It would have been their collective and individual decision. That is what real and true collectivism is. It is letting human beings make their own decisions after being given all sides of the argument and letting them battle out their differences without regard to deadlines, ideologies or agendas. If given enough time, the truth will always reveal itself and lead us where we need to go.

Part IV
Flattening the Pyramid

Similar to the first commandment of the Ten Commandments and what Jesus viewed as the greatest commandment to love God with all our heart, mind, strength and soul, the first paragraph of the Declaration of Independence and the first Article of the U.N.'s Universal Declaration of Human Rights all recognize the command for us to view one another as equals at the energetic level of mind where our consciousness of God in the form of our human consciousness of true and false resides (aka our conscience). Jesus, the founders of America and the U.N.'s Commission on Human Rights obviously did not consult with one another and come up with similar ideas and documents. What they did do was to take a realistic and honest approach towards themselves and their fellow men and women. They knocked down the structures that have us putting one another into categories of human beings and began their analysis from the foundation floor. They recognized that we are not separate and distinct physical bodies that need to be objectified and categorized for purposes of a command and control structure that ends up enslaving the minds of us all. Rather, we are all interconnected naturally through a spirit of life that infuses each one of us with the desire to learn and grow at our own pace in an atmosphere of freedom and equality for all. Human beings can argue over whether or not there is a God but in a sense it doesn't matter. Unless God clearly manifests in our physical world in a way that convinces everyone of its existence, then each one of us is required to deal with what we know to be real and true. Denial of reality and truth as a means of gaining what is in one's own self interest is humanity's sin. It is the original sin of Adam and Eve that continues to dog us because we have not had the courage to look at ourselves realistically on both an individual and a collective basis. We all have too much riding on the lie. Selfishness and greed is not about money. Selfishness and greed is the inability to understand a person's suffering because you have not suffered in a similar way. Money is the root of all evil because it is the tool used to gain power within the animal-mirrored organizational structures humanity has put in place in this physical world as a means of maintaining order.

I saw an interview with Milton Friedman, the author of *Capitalism and Freedom*, where he callously explains that capitalism is a system that is overwhelmingly getting great results but it's not perfect and there are cases where people will get hurt, but that is true in any system.[6] Is that true? Have we ever come together as a global community and tried to put our heads together to come up with a system that works for everyone? Currently, we have capitalism that has devolved into a form of cronyism that favors the rich, a corrupted form of socialism called communism and dictatorships of one kind or another. Certainly these are not the only systems a conscious population of seven billion plus people can come up with. What he and other people like him need to ask themselves is whether they would like to be one of the people who gets hurt in these systems. It is easy for the haves of this world to be so callous and to justify their callousness by proclaiming they have worked hard and deserve to profit from it. Most of us work hard yet we have to do it in a system that views us as tools to a great extent. When anonymous shareholders demanding profits above all else become the company owners, then employees become just another number on the balance sheet. Jesus said, "A hired man, who is not a shepherd and whose sheep are not his own, sees a wolf coming and leaves the sheep and runs away, and the wolf catches and scatters them. This is because he works for pay and has no concern for the sheep."

It is quite illustrative that America's service industries have risen in direct proportion to the decline of its manufacturing sector. America quit producing as a country because corporations sent all the manufacturing jobs overseas where labor was cheap, saying they had to in order to compete. They said they had to answer to their shareholders - invisible shareholders whose only stake in their companies was their monthly dividend statements. When shareholders dictate policy, it almost requires that the executives in power be cutthroat and willing to do anything to make a buck for the shareholders' pockets because that is the motive of shareholders: to receive as much money as possible back for their investment. That is why China now poses such a threat. They are smarter in a corrupt system. They are long range thinkers. They are patient. They are willing to do and buy whoever it takes to gain military and technology secrets to gain an upper hand. America's politicians are greedy and short sighted. They come from the same population of people as the HR manager in my workplace who viewed money as the sole incentive of American workers and considered companies who believe in nurturing the personal and professional growth of their employees as cults. She is representative of where America went wrong. It got too greedy. We were the most powerful nation, oddly enough, when our taxes were high and we were paying workers a living wage. In the 1950's and after, we had the advantage of working in a capitalist system with a foundation of people who knew the difference between right and wrong. Business deals could be done with a handshake because both parties trusted one another to do right by each other. We caved into evil at the hand of the almighty dollar. China could produce products cheaper by using slave labor and we convinced ourselves we couldn't compete. I wonder what would have happened if we had established some ground rules that companies would not let their policies be guided by the shareholders' monthly statements. What if we had decided that we wanted a nation of people who could live well; not hand over all our wealth to the one percent on the top? I think the result would have been huge amounts of wealth flowing horizontally, instead of vertically, because it would have forced us to use our minds to come up with creative solutions to compete. Creativity has enormous power because it flows from truth and reality. We see things the way God sees them. The universal power that used logic and mathematics to create the working pieces of this universe would have been put to use in our nation. America would have been unstoppable. Everyone would have benefited. Who knows. We might have made a discovery that allowed us to create a car that was better than the Hondas and Toyotas at a lower cost. We'll never know because we caved under a false consciousness that told us in order to compete we needed to stoop to the levels of immoral governments willing to exploit their people to gain an upper hand in the marketplace. The result is that we are now operating in a system in which many of us have no stake. It is a system where quotas, numbers, time cards and sales figures are valued and the human being is merely the machine generating them. Machines have no inherent value. When the machine breaks or becomes outdated, it is simply replaced by another one and expensed on the balance sheet as depreciation or loss. However, like the Israelites who wanted to return to slavery in Egypt, we are unable to even consider the possibility of changing the system because we have all built our lives within it. All we can see is what we would lose if we were to dismantle the status quo of our existence. Like the Israelites, we are unable to see what we could create in a world devoid of the existing structures.

The wilderness is so frightening when viewed by the constructs of minds that have been brought up and shaped by the external structures currently in place. At least within the structures, we know what we know. There is a certain amount of certainty by which we can create a course for our lives. Change is so terrifying because it puts us in the zone of uncertainty. It requires us to have faith in ourselves and that is the scariest faith of all. I think that is why the U.N., Moses and America's founders all came up with a similar set of rules that value each of us individually. Their values if internalized by each of us individually would ensure that no one gets left behind. The Milton Friedmans of this world would become dinosaurs because these values prevent any person from being viewed as acceptable collateral damage by another human being. They put the burden on each of us individually to come up with solutions that brings the whole of humanity into the Garden of Eden. They are written in stone as the rights of every man and woman entering the promised land this earth was meant to be when it was created with the resources to provide for all and not just by the lucky few who have perched themselves at the top of man-made structures modeled on the animal kingdom.

Conclusion

I think the most astonishing fact I learned from reading the transcripts of the Nuremberg trials is how few men it took to take over a country and turn it into a hell on earth with the consent and cooperation of the populace. The German people knew who Hitler was and what he wanted to accomplish. Volume 1 of Mein Kampf was published in 1925 and Volume 2 in 1926, more than a decade before World War II. In it, Hitler makes clear his hatred for the Jews and his belief that they were the cause of all of society's ills. Even still, he was elected to office with much of the upper-class Jewish vote because they identified with him on a social class level. They thought they were exempt from his vitriolic hatred. He was clear about who he was and what he wanted to do but because he promised the German people jobs, they followed him through the gates of Hell. By the time they glimpsed the society they themselves helped him create, they were all too fearful to do anything about it. They could have made different choices – harder choices – and worked through their country's problems in more constructive ways than putting a demented dictator in charge, but he was charismatic and told them what they wanted to hear. He also gave them much of what they wanted, but at what price? I can answer that. The price of their humanity.

Maybe government, that Eleanor Roosevelt assumed was a necessary foundation upon which to build a set of guaranteed human rights, is inherently evil because it is a group of individuals telling other individuals how they should live their lives when each individual has the knowledge within to take care of themselves. We no longer have control over what our government does. What we have are career politicians who have bought themselves lifetime appointments. The men and women in our three branches of government are among the richest people in America. Every day I read about legislation that was passed or executive orders that were signed when no one was looking. That is why our skies will soon be littered with drones watching our every move, toddlers are getting patted down by Homeland Security at the airport, our food choices in the marketplace are becoming smaller and smaller, our emails are being monitored without warrants and whistle blowers are getting punished for merely stating the truth.

I believe hell is running out of options in a universe of limitless possibilities. The Jews in the concentration camps were in hell. Having our freedom of choice taken away is a form of hell because it deprives us of our ability to self-determine our own lives. We come into the world alone and go out alone for a reason. I believe the reason for that is because each of us has our own individual lessons to learn in order to advance to the next level of our growth in an ever expanding, changing and evolving realm of energy directed by the stream of consciousness that exists in heaven and on

Earth. Heaven is not a place we go to. Neither is hell. Heaven and hell are creations of consciousness. When we make our minds conform to external environments that have negated the positive energy of creation in favor of maintaining the status quo, we destroy our own positive life force of growth and creation. It is why we continue the cycles of growth, decay, death and growth again in ourselves and in our world.

While I was undergoing the mobbing in my workplace, I began losing my grip on reality. I didn't know what was happening to me at the time and the fear and paranoia it instilled in me lasted for a very long time afterward. Now I know what the crux of it was. No matter what I said, no matter what I did, no matter who I went to with my concerns, it didn't matter. The mob had made its choice to banish me. No lie was big enough and no action on their part outrageous enough to achieve their goal. I was up against a brick wall in which I had no voice. I had become a pest in the form of an ant to be squashed. The humanity in myself that I cherished did not exist in the eyes of the mob. I was a non-entity who did not know she was a non-entity. In the words of Nietzche, I was looking into the abyss and it was looking back at me ready to consume me. If not for my ability to listen to my intuition and follow it even though it meant giving up the job I loved with all my soul, I would have fallen into their trap and the outcome would have been dire. I have come to call that intuition that saved me God. Other people call it nature and still others call it human spirit. Whatever it is called, it should be valued and nurtured in all of us. I believe that is what declarations, commandments and constitutions like the ones discussed in this book try to do by changing our focus from the external, physical manifestation of our humanity to the inner reality where our human consciousness exists.

Humanity has never given itself a chance. We have never placed our collective focus on alleviating human suffering. We have accepted it as part of the human condition. We have never placed our collective focus on alleviating poverty and hunger. We have let our governments take care of it piecemeal. We have never placed our collective focus on achieving equality for all. We have let systems that value competition pit us against one another. We have never placed our collective focus on abolishing illogical reasoning that sees some difference in the way a female and a male should be treated when the only thing that separates them is their physical form. We have let culture define them in terms of male and female roles. We have never placed our collective focus on abolishing all forms of bigotry in the human race. We have let our leaders legislate it for us. Like the Israelites, we have not wanted to hear from God. We have not wanted to listen to our own human spirit that clearly sees the whole of humanity as consisting of all its individual human parts. To me, that is what true collectivism is. It is not what China and the former Soviet Union redefined it as in pursuit of protecting their collective power interests. It is letting reality and truth guide us individually and collectively toward our future. It is breaking down the man-made barriers that were constructed in a bygone era when men and women lived with an animal consciousness of survival in a hostile physical environment and replacing them with beliefs and structures that respect the human consciousness that binds us all together through birth.

Like a computer program with a bug, we must logically dig down and through the false assumptions we have accepted as truth in order to get to the foundation floor of our humanity where it is clear and logical that (1) Birth entitles each of us to equal dignity, rights and freedom; (2) Every human being is individually born with reason and a conscience, and; (3) Our individual reason and conscience can be used to act towards one another in a spirit of brotherhood. Only then will the words inked on our constitutions, declarations and mission statements become living truth within the minds of each and human being they touch. Only then will the man-made structures and belief systems like competition and hierarchy be seen for the selfserving game they are in a world where all men and women are equal through a birthright of reason and conscience. Only then will lasting change worth believing in take place.

Universal Declaration Of Human Rights

Article I
All human beings are born free and equal in dignity and rights. They are endowed with reason and conscience and should act towards one another in a spirit of brotherhood.

Article 2
Everyone is entitled to all the rights and freedoms set forth in this Declaration, without distinction of any kind, such as race, colour, sex, language, religion, political or other opinion, national or social origin, property, birth or other status. Furthermore, no distinction shall be made on the basis of the political, jurisdictional or international status of the country or territory to which a person belongs, whether it be independent, trust, non-selfgoverning or under any other limitation of sovereignty.

Article 3
Everyone has the right to life, liberty and security of person.

Article 4
No one shall be held in slavery or servitude; slavery and the slave trade shall be prohibited in all their forms.

Article 5 No one shall be subjected to torture or to cruel, inhuman or degrading treatment or punishment.

Article 6
Everyone has the right to recognition everywhere as a person before the law.

Article 7 All are equal before the law and are entitled without any discrimination to equal protection of the law. All are entitled to equal protection against any discrimination in violation of this Declaration and against any incitement to such discrimination.

Article 8
Everyone has the right to an effective remedy by the competent national tribunals for acts violating the fundamental rights granted him by the constitution or by law.

Article 9
No one shall be subjected to arbitrary arrest, detention or exile.

Article 10
Everyone is entitled in full equality to a fair and public hearing by an independent and impartial tribunal, in the determination of his rights and obligations and of any criminal charge against him.

Article 11
1. Everyone charged with a penal offence has the right to be presumed innocent until proved guilty according to law in a public trial at which he has had all the guarantees necessary for his defence.

2. No one shall be held guilty of any penal offence on account of any act or omission which did not constitute a penal offence, under national or international law, at the time when it was committed. Nor shall a heavier penalty be imposed than the one that was applicable at the time the penal offence was committed.

Article 12
No one shall be subjected to arbitrary interference with his privacy, family, home or correspondence, nor to attacks upon his honour and reputation. Everyone has the right to the protection of the law against such interference or attacks.

Article 13
1. Everyone has the right to freedom of movement and residence within the borders of each State.

2.   Everyone has the right to leave any country, including his own, and to return to his country.

Article 14

1. Everyone has the right to seek and to enjoy in other countries asylum from persecution.

2. This right may not be invoked in the case of prosecutions genuinely arising from non-political crimes or from acts contrary to the purposes and principles of the United Nations.

Article 15

1. Everyone has the right to a nationality.

2. No one shall be arbitrarily deprived of his nationality nor denied the right to change his nationality.

Article 16

1. Men and women of full age, without any limitation due to race, nationality or religion, have the right to marry and to found a family. They are entitled to equal rights as to marriage, during marriage and at its dissolution.

2, Marriage shall be entered into only with the free and full consent of the intending spouses.

3. The family is the natural and fundamental group unit of society and is entitled to protection by society and the State.

Article 17

1. Everyone has the right to own property alone as well as in association with others.

2. No one shall be arbitrarily deprived of his property.

Article 18

Everyone has the right to freedom of thought, conscience and religion; this right includes freedom to change his religion or belief, and freedom, either alone or in community with others and in public or private, to manifest his religion or belief in teaching, practice, worship and observance.

Article 19

Everyone has the right to freedom of opinion and expression; this right includes freedom to hold opinions without interference and to seek, receive and impart information and ideas through any media and regardless of frontiers.

Article 20

1. Everyone has the right to freedom of peaceful assembly and association.

2. No one may be compelled to belong to an association.

Article 21

1.Everyone has the right to take part in the government of his country, directly or through freely chosen representatives.

2. Everyone has the right to equal access to public service in his country.

3. The will of the people shall be the basis of the authority of government; this will shall be expressed in periodic and genuine elections which shall be by universal and equal suffrage and shall be held by secret vote or by equivalent free voting procedures.

Article 22
Everyone, as a member of society, has the right to social security and is entitled to realization, through national effort and international cooperation and in accordance with the organization and resources of each State, of the economic, social and cultural rights indispensable for his dignity and the free development of his personality.

Article 23
1. Everyone has the right to work, to free choice of employment, to just and favourable conditions of work and to protection against unemployment.

2. Everyone, without any discrimination, has the right to equal pay for equal work.

3. Everyone who works has the right to just and favourable remuneration ensuring for himself and his family an existence worthy of human dignity, and supplemented, if necessary, by other means of social protection.

4. Everyone has the right to form and to join trade unions for the protection of his interests.

Article 24
Everyone has the right to rest and leisure, including reasonable limitation of working hours and periodic holidays with pay.

Article 25
1. Everyone has the right to a standard of living adequate for the health and well-being of himself and of his family, including food, clothing, housing and medical care and necessary social services, and the right to security in the event of unemployment, sickness, disability, widowhood, old age or other lack of livelihood in circumstances beyond his

control.

2. Motherhood and childhood are entitled to special care and assistance. All children, whether born in or out of wedlock, shall enjoy the same social protection.

Article 26

1. Everyone has the right to education. Education shall be free, at least in the elementary and fundamental stages. Elementary education shall be compulsory. Technical and professional education shall be made generally available and higher education shall be equally accessible to all on the basis of merit.

2. Education shall be directed to the full development of the human personality and to the strengthening of respect for human rights and fundamental freedoms. It shall promote understanding, tolerance and friendship among all nations, racial or religious groups, and shall further the activities of the United Nations for the maintenance of peace.

3. Parents have a prior right to choose the kind of education that shall be given to their children.

Article 27

1. Everyone has the right freely to participate in the cultural life of the community, to enjoy the arts and to share in scientific advancement and its benefits.

2. Everyone has the right to the protection of the moral and material interests resulting from any scientific, literary or artistic production of which he is the author.

Article 28

Everyone is entitled to a social and international order in which the rights and freedoms set forth in this Declaration can be fully realized.

Article 29

1. Everyone has duties to the community in which alone the free and full development of his personality is possible.

2. In the exercise of his rights and freedoms, everyone shall be subject only to such limitations as are determined by law solely for the purpose of securing due recognition and respect for the rights and freedoms of others and of meeting the just requirements of morality, public order and the general welfare in a democratic society.

3. These rights and freedoms may in no case be exercised contrary to the purposes and principles of the United Nations.

Article 30

Nothing in this Declaration may be interpreted as implying for any State, group or person any right to engage in any activity or to perform any act aimed at the destruction of any of the rights and freedoms set forth herein.

BIBLIOGRAPHY

Unless otherwise indicated in these endnotes, all quotations from the Bible have been taken from the online versions of the King James Bible and the Bible in Basic English. Introduction

1.   Sears, J. F. (2008). Eleanor Roosevelt And The Universal Declaration Of Human Rights. Franklin and Eleanor Roosevelt Institute (FERI). Retrieved from www.erooseveltudhr.org.

2.   Ibid, pg. 7

3.   Ibid, pg. 8

4.   Genesis 3:11-13

5.   Leidner, G. (2013). The founding fathers: quotes, quips, and speeches.

6.   Johnson, J. (Director). (2006). The One Percent [Motion picture]. USA: Wise and Good Film/HBO Documentary Films

www.ingramcontent.com/pod-product-compliance
Lightning Source LLC
Chambersburg PA
CBHW060644280326
41933CB00012B/2146